Wonderful Things are Happening!

Dorothy Rieke

The Bookmark
Santa Clarita, California

Copyright 2002 by Ann Beals

All rights reserved under the International
and Pan-American Copyright Convention

ISBN 0-930227-42-5

Published by
The Bookmark
Post Office Box 801143
Santa Clarita, California 91380

WONDERFUL THINGS ARE HAPPENING!

When the coming of Christ Jesus was foretold by Isaiah, it was said of him, " . . . and his name shall be called Wonderful." In speaking of the appearing of the Christ Science, Mrs. Eddy asks, "Is he wonderful?" She replies, "His works prove him. He giveth power, peace, and holiness; he exalteth the lowly; he giveth liberty to the captive, health to the sick, salvation from sin to the sinner — and overcometh the world!" (*Miscellaneous Writings*)

After over a hundred years of this Christ Science in action, it is only fitting that we contemplate the wonderful things which are taking place as a result of the teachings of Christ Jesus and the discovery and the establishment of the Science of Christianity by Mary Baker Eddy.

One night, following a Wednesday evening testimony meeting, a friend of mine made a statement to a friend of hers. She said with great positiveness and conviction in her voice, "Don't be concerned about anything — wonderful things are happening!" She was so emphatic in making her statement that another lady overheard it. On the way home, she started to think about this positive, joyous approach. She realized that this positive, joyous attitude had certainly not been the attitude that she had been entertaining. She had been very much concerned for many reasons — an incurable disease which had been growing steadily worse, a business which had failed, and her son who was in a danger zone in a war torn country. She asked herself, "How can I say I am unconcerned?" The answer came just as if it were God speaking to her. "Because God is all there is, there is absolutely nothing to be concerned about."

Wonderful Things Are Happening!

Then she asked herself, "How can I rejoice and say that wonderful things are happening?" The answer came, "Because God is all there is, and He is expressing Himself. The results have to be wonderful."

That night on the way home, she determined that no matter what was manifested in her body, or in her affairs, she was going to refuse to be concerned. Instead, she was going to rejoice consistently that wonderful things were taking place. She realized that the basis for such a positive, joyous approach was scientific because she was truly convinced that God is All, and that God is really expressing Himself.

She stood steadfast in her practice of this scientific, positive, joyous attitude. As a result she was very quickly healed, and her business became far more successful than it had ever been.

This lady's daughter-in-law was ill. The daughter-in-law came to the mother-in-law for help. She, too, had been concerned about many things. She had been concerned about her own illness, and problems in the schoolroom where she was a teacher. And she had been concerned about the young man in the danger zone, because he was her husband. The mother-in-law shared this positive, joyous approach with her daughter-in-law, and told her of the wonderful things that had come to pass because she had steadfastly put this attitude to work. The daughter-in-law decided that she, too, regardless of what came up in her body or in her affairs, would consistently and steadfastly refuse to be concerned. But, instead, would rejoice that wonderful things were happening. As a result she was healed. Her husband was brought home to a spot so close he didn't even seem to be in the Army anymore. Everything worked out harmoniously in her teaching.

There's one other incident I must share with you. One day a little girl came to this teacher and said, "I have a little friend who wants to take her life. Her father and mother don't love each other any more. They don't love her. Her home is awful, and she really

WONDERFUL THINGS ARE HAPPENING!

wants to commit suicide. What can I say to her?" The teacher, of course, was just full of this positive, joyous way of thinking, so she shared it with the little girl in terms that she could understand. She said, "You tell your little friend that no matter how bad things seem to be at home, just because God loves her, He will make wonderful things take place. However, she must know this and have faith in it, and rejoice in it." In about a week's time, the little girl returned to the teacher and said, "I have a confession to make. I was the little girl who wanted to commit suicide. But I went home and I told my father and mother what you told me, and they love each other now, and they love me, and home is wonderful, and I wouldn't take my life for anything." So the school teacher told the mother-in-law, and in turn she gave a testimony, and my friend heard how this positive, joyous statement that she had shared, had reached out and blessed six individuals, because they had all put it to work.

There are two very important conclusions that I have drawn from this testimony. First, it didn't make any difference whether the individual was an old-time Christian Scientist who had been studying for years and had become discouraged, or one who was so brand new in Christian Science she didn't even know she was a Scientist — yet the positive, joyous attitude healed. Secondly, it didn't make any difference whether the problem was a business problem, an incurable disease, location in the danger zone, an illness, problems connected with the schoolroom, or a problem of human relationships — that same positive, joyous attitude healed. And the healing is still going on. I have shared this testimony all over the United States and, in fact, in any country where I could give testimonies. And reports are still coming back to me from all over the world telling me, "I, too, am standing steadfast in rejoicing that there is absolutely nothing to be concerned about, and that wonderful things are happening." And then they tell me about healings they have experienced as a result of their sharing this positive, joyous approach.

WONDERFUL THINGS ARE HAPPENING!

The last time my husband lectured throughout Germany and Switzerland in the German language, we spent a month in Munich in preparation for the German lecture. I prayed that God would use me in a way whereby I could truly bless. Well, He certainly did! God told me to have this testimony translated into German so that I could share it on Wednesday nights. A wonderful Christian Scientist translated it for me and coached me so that I could read it properly. Every Wednesday night, I would read my testimony in German. At the close of each meeting, the German people would rush up to me to thank me for that wonderful testimony and, of course, they would speak very rapidly, and I didn't know what they were saying. Never for an instant would they have thought that anyone who could read such beautiful German so well, couldn't be able to understand them. Then I would tell them in German that I spoke very little German, but that I spoke a little. From that point on, we would get along famously. And you know, I'm still receiving thrilling reports from Germany about the fact that wonderful things are taking place, because individuals refuse to be concerned.

One of the most thrilling experiences I had was in a little town in Switzerland. My husband was to give his last lecture in German on a Sunday afternoon. People came not only from that part of Switzerland, but many came down from Germany. The lecture was to be held in the ballroom of the hotel. But please don't picture the ballroom as you would find it in a hotel in Detroit — this building was over two hundred years old. It was one of those picturesque old buildings of brick and mortar painted white, held together with pieces of black wood. Long before all the people were in the ballroom, the owner of the hotel was wringing his hands. He said, "We can't let any more people in. The building is too old; it will collapse." My husband solved the problem by starting the lecture early, and by giving a second lecture. Because these people had never had such an experience and didn't know what to do about it, I found myself directing the situation. And I ended up outside the building during the first lecture.

Wonderful Things Are Happening!

As I stood rejoicing about so many people coming to the lecture, a lady approached me. She said they had come a great distance. The rest of the family, all except her mother, were in hearing the first lecture. The mother was unable to walk. They had brought her, knowing that she would not be able to hear the lecture, but they thought Mr. Rieke might be able to speak with her. However, she said that by the time the second lecture was over, it would be far too late for them to start home. Thus, she knew that her mother would not be able to talk with him, but would I come and talk with her? Believe it or not, I talked with that lady for twenty minutes in German. I said things in German I had never dreamed I would be able to say. I had the copy of the testimony in my purse, which I had been reading at the services. I gave it to her. I told her that she, too, would be healed. You can imagine the joy that was mine when she returned the testimony along with a letter telling me that she had been completely healed.

The first basic metaphysical law underlying the statement, "I'm not concerned about anything — wonderful things are happening," is not a formula, nor is it a Pollyanna attitude on seeing only the good in spite of the bad. The statement, "I am not concerned about anything," is based upon the most important of all metaphysical laws — *the law that God is All*. It is because of the allness of God that there is absolutely nothing to be concerned about. Let's think about the allness of God for a few minutes. Listen to some of the statements that God Himself makes, as found in Isaiah: "I am God, and there is none else; I am God, and there is none like me." "I am the first, and I am the last and beside me there is no God." Mrs. Eddy attributes great importance to the law of metaphysics, that God is All. In *Unity of Good*, she speaks of it as a self-proved proposition and an incontestable point in divine Science. In *No and Yes*, she states: "God's law is in three words, 'I am All'; and this perfect law is ever present to rebuke any claim of another law."

Wonderful Things Are Happening!

I find great inspiration in contemplating God's allness from the statement found in the Christian Science textbook, *Science and Health with Key to the Scriptures*; where Mrs. Eddy says, "Unfathomable Mind is expressed. The depth, breadth, height, might, majesty, and glory of infinite Love fill all space." I am sure all of you have in individual ways been enabling yourselves to comprehend this tremendous infinitude of God. Somehow, I seem to feel deeply His allness when I say, "Why I'm right in the midst of God. Fifty billion miles all around me there's nothing but God. Fifty billion miles beyond that and beyond that, there is nothing but God. Therefore, there is absolutely nothing to touch me but God. There is nothing to influence me, condition me, govern or control me, but God!"

In the textbook, we read, "Since God is All, there is no room for His unlikeness." There cannot be both God and an accident, war, earthquake, tornado, or violence of any description. There is only God. There cannot be both God and heart trouble, tumor, cancer, palsy, epilepsy, colds, sickness, or disease of any description. There is just God.

There cannot be both God and hatred, fear, criticism, resentment, rebellion, worry, or sin of any kind. There is just God. There cannot be both God and even a belief in error, because this law rebukes even a claim or a belief contrary to God's allness. There is no claim or belief, no dream, no illusion. There is just God. How does the law of God's allness rebuke even a claim or a belief of another law? It is because unfathomable, infinite, eternal, divine Mind is All, and there is no other mind, no mortal mind, to entertain even a claim or a belief of something opposed to God. There is just God, divine Mind. How wonderful it is that no matter what the error, we understand it to be completely nonexistent, utterly impossible, because of the ever-presence of the allness of God. So, when we say, "I'm not concerned about anything," we actually mean that because of the allness of God, there is absolutely nothing to be concerned about. It was because of the allness of God that it

WONDERFUL THINGS ARE HAPPENING!

was impossible for a woman to have an incurable disease, impossible for a man to be in a danger zone, impossible for there to be problems in a schoolroom, impossible for a husband and wife not to love each other, impossible for a business career to be ruined, and impossible for a little girl to take her life.

A young lady who was working in an office alone, suddenly found herself in the throes of severe pain, and realized that she had lost her power of speech, and that she was losing consciousness. All she could think of was God, and she repeated the word "God" mentally as she lost consciousness. Some time later, as she started to regain consciousness, she was again aware only of God. Finally, she could say the word, but nothing else came, so she repeated the word "God" until she could say "God is." She found her speech and thought becoming clearer and repeated, "God is" until she could say, "God is All." She was so grateful and so joyous in being able to realize, acknowledge, and voice the allness of God, that shortly she found herself manifesting only perfection. Her healing was complete, and it was permanent.

Oh, isn't it wonderful that just because of the allness of God, we don't have to be concerned about anything? By the way, what are you concerned about? Your health, your family, your church, your supply, the state of the nation, world affairs? I am asking all of you to repeat with me, "I am not concerned about anything; because God is All, there is nothing to be concerned about."

God Expressing Himself

The second basic metaphysical law underlying our positive, joyous statement is that God is expressing Himself. It is thrilling to realize that God, who is All-in-all, is a *divinely active* God. Just contemplating God as Life, we see so readily that there is never any interruption to *divinely active* being. Contemplating God as Mind, we see that there could never be such a thing as a divine Mind that is not thinking, knowing, understanding, comprehending, and expressing. Contemplating God as Love — why, it is impossible to think of God as Love, and not realize that He is ever *actively* loving His perfect creation. Just listen to the *activity* of God as expressed by just one Psalm: "Who coverest thyself with light as with a garment: who stretchest out the heavens like a curtain: Who layeth the beams of his chambers in the waters: Who maketh the clouds his chariot: who walketh upon the wings of the wind. . . Who laid the foundations of the earth; . . He sendeth the springs into the valleys, which run among the hills. They give drink to every beast of the field: . . He watereth the hills from his chambers: the earth is satisfied with the fruit of thy works. He causeth the grass to grow for the cattle, and herb for the service of man: that he may bring forth food out of the earth. . . The trees of the Lord are full of sap; the cedars of Lebanon, which He hath planted; . . . He appointed the moon for seasons: the sun knoweth his going down . . . thou openest thine hand, they are filled with good. He looketh on the earth, and it trembleth: he toucheth the hills, and they smoke." No wonder David exclaims: "Lord, how manifold are thy works! In wisdom hast Thou made them all; the earth is full of thy riches." And so it is because we have a *divinely active* God, that wonderful things are happening. It is because our perfect, omnipotent, omnipresent, omniscient God is expressing all His qualities in perfect balance, that wonderful things are taking place.

Now, this one and only divinely active God does all the doing in the universe. Not only does He do all the creating, but all the knowing, all the understanding, all the expressing. He does all the regulating, all the governing, all the controlling. He does all the relating, the associating, the environing. The definition of Mind in the 'Glossary' of *Science and Health* reads: "Deity, which outlines but is not outlined." God doing all the planning, all the outlining, is a very important basic truth that we must accept in our expecta-

WONDERFUL THINGS ARE HAPPENING!

tion of wonderful things happening. I doubt if there is any one statement I have made more often than this one — "God's plan for man is in operation, and there is no other power or presence that can interfere with it." I wish to discuss this statement with you in relation to wonderful things taking place.

There isn't a one of us who, at some time during a year, doesn't need to let that glorious truth operate in his experience — to find the right job, select the right apartment, buy the right car, choose the right university, join the right church, accept the right church assignments, take the right vacation, marry the right person. In making any one of these decisions, we must rejoice consistently that God's plan for us is in operation. To be absolutely sure that it is God who is doing the outlining, and not me, myself, there are four basic truths I love to contemplate, comprehend, and rejoice in. These truths were unfolded to me at a time when I thought I had a problem that was beyond solution. I couldn't see how even God could have an answer. It was at that time that I took a little boy and his mother sailing. It was the three-year old child's first experience in a sailboat. He was impressed by the expanse of water, and he was besieging his mother with questions. "Is the water over my head? Is it over brother's head? Over your head?" "Yes, it is over Daddy's head," the mother replied. The little fellow thought for a moment, and then with a look of absolute confidence, he announced: "But it isn't over God's head."

That night, when I had an opportunity to be alone, I went out of doors, sat under the stars and prayed. I knew that what the little boy had said was a message from God to me — that my problem wasn't over God's head. I turned wholeheartedly to my heavenly Father. I let divine Mind talk, and I listened. It was then that those four precious, but powerful points, were revealed to me:

First, from *Science and Health*: *"Soul has infinite resources with which to bless mankind."* Don't ever start working on a problem with a limited sense of things, such as "Jobs are few and far between." Or, "There are just no eligible men my age who are Christian Scientists." Or, "There is only one school for me, but I don't know which one." Begin with the infinitude of God's goodness. Remember that His resources are infinite. The possibilities for income are beyond measure. The possibilities of employment are infinite. The possibilities for the right place to live are infinite. Opportunities to serve are infinite. Because all the resources are of Soul, God, they are infinite, boundless, unlimited, immeasurable, ever-present, and ever-available. Now, these wonderful resources of God do not lie idle. He uses His "infinite resources" to bless you. No matter what your need might be, it is tremendously thrilling to start out with the realization of the infinite possibilities whereby your heavenly Father might bless you. Of course, because the resources are God's, they must all be necessarily beautiful, harmonious, wonderful, good, and perfect in every respect. Rejoice that you are rich. You have inherited the kingdom. In Luke, we read, "Son, thou art ever with me, and all that I have is thine."

Second: *Divine Mind, the all-knowing intelligence, knows which resources best meet the needs of every individual.* Jesus tells us, "Your heavenly Father knoweth that ye have need of all these things." Isn't it wonderful that we can trust God, and know that His planning is far beyond anything that we could humanly plan? God, divine Mind, employs His resources for man in perfect wisdom; and therefore, for one who understands this, no avenue is blocked, no right desire unsatisfied, no need unprovided. It is at this point of the demonstration where we must stand steadfast in refusing to outline. We must rely completely upon the decisions of our heavenly Father as to what is best for us. We must not even be guilty of saying, "Heavenly Father, Thy will be done — but I just kind of hope it will work out my way." No, we must pray without reservation, " . . . not my will, but thine, be done." Sometimes in order to be absolutely certain that I am letting God do all the planning, I will pray this way: "God, I don't care whether I dig gold in

WONDERFUL THINGS ARE HAPPENING!

Alaska, lasso cattle in Argentina, scrub floors in a Benevolent Association, or take in washing in Timbuktu. All I ask, Father, is that Your plan for me be in operation." And then I rejoice that it is God's plan, and God's plan only, that is in operation, and absolutely nothing can interfere with it. Oh, with what complete assurance, freedom, and confidence, can we face the future knowing that God is caring for us in every experience.

Third, from *Science and Health*: *"Love inspires, illumines, designates, and leads the way."* Isn't this a wonderful thought? So often you will hear an individual say, "But how am I to know what is God's plan for me?" Or, "How am I to know what footsteps to take?" Or "God may know, but I certainly don't." This wonderful statement from the textbook guarantees that man cannot help but know the right steps to take and the right decisions to make.

It is not a case of God knowing all the answers, and man being in the dark. God is forever pouring His thoughts and judgments into our waiting consciousness, thus inspiring us with the right ideas. It is the great light of Truth which illumines our pathway so completely that we cannot help but see the right turn to take, or the right decision to make. Moreover, divine Mind literally points out to us which is best of all His infinite opportunities. And what's more, your heavenly Father takes you by the hand and leads the way. Thus, anyone rejoicing that "Love inspires, illumines, designates, and leads the way," can't escape doing the thing that is right for him to do. So how do we know what is God's will and what is not? That is the beauty of Love's inspiration, illumination, and designation. When God's purpose is revealed, the way is so clear, so certain, that not only are we sure of it, but we are led, impelled, compelled to take it.

It is at this point in our demonstration where we must refuse to become discouraged if we see no signs or have no leadings. Even though we haven't had any indication that things are happen-

WONDERFUL THINGS ARE HAPPENING!

ing, yet we know that they *are*. Don't forget, our God is a *divinely active* God, ever expressing Himself. Therefore, now and always, wonderful things are happening. And regardless of whether we see any evidence of it or not, let us continue in our rejoicing that *now* God's plan is in operation. Right *now* wonderful things are taking place. Why, right now God can be opening the way for that individual in California to come to your home and offer to buy that property you want to sell. Why, right at this instant God may be working things out in New York City whereby an organization will find it possible to ask you to fill a position that is far beyond anything you have ever dreamed of. Discouragement closes the door on illumination and inspiration. But courage and confidence that wonderful things are happening, leave all the doors wide open for wonderful things to happen, and for us to be aware of God's guidance.

A young man had worked several weeks along these lines in order to find just the right job. Nothing had developed that was in keeping with his talents and abilities. But you know, he was so sure, so certain, so positive God's plan was in operation, and that wonderful things were happening, that he was not the least bit unhappy, or disturbed, or worried, or fearful. One day he was impelled to go to a nearby town and apply for a position with an organization that he hadn't even thought of before. Well, they had a position for him, and it was far more wonderful than anything he had dreamed of. After they had guaranteed him the position, they said to him, "How did you happen to come today? If you had come yesterday, the position wouldn't have been open yet. If you had come tomorrow, we would have already filled it with one of our employees. How did you happen to come today?" The young man's reply was, "Only God knows. All I know was that I was impelled to come." However, this young man told me later that he realized that it was because he had stood steadfast in his joy and his certainty that wonderful things were happening that he was able to hear the voice of God, able to feel the directive impulse. He said that if he

WONDERFUL THINGS ARE HAPPENING!

had become worried or discouraged or unhappy, he wouldn't have been in tune with the infinite, and he would probably still be looking for a job.

Fourth: *Divine Principle puts God's plan for man into operation, and there is no other power or presence to interfere with it one iota.* This is the last point, but it is a tremendously important one. It is because of the operation of Principle which is the law, the way, the order of things, that there is absolutely no possibility of there being any other law to interfere with the operation of God's plan. Referring to this omnipotent power of divine Principle, Mrs. Eddy says, "Let us open our affections to the Principle that moves all in harmony, — from the falling of a sparrow to the rolling of a world." There can be no circumstances so great that Principle cannot encompass it. There can be no need so insignificant that Principle cannot provide for it. Let us follow Mrs. Eddy's admonition to open our affection to Principle. Let us love, worship, and adore that Supreme Power which holds the universe in place. Let us revere the law which annihilates the possibility of there being a law to the contrary. There can be no medical law to interfere with God's plan for you; no law of lack or excess; no law of false theology; even a lack of education cannot interfere with God's plan for man, because the infinite power of divine Principle is putting God's plan into operation. Before the presence of divine Principle, all intolerance, bigotry, misunderstanding, misconceptions, and even human opinions, become as nothing, as a thing of naught. Remember that it is divine Principle that does all the placing, all the arranging, all the planning, all the relating and associating, all the organizing, all the being, all the motivating. No wonder there is nothing to interfere with God's plan.

One day I had been working particularly with the second point. Refusing to outline, I had just finished praying, "Heavenly Father, I don't care whether I dig gold in Alaska, lasso cattle in Argentina, scrub floors in a Benevolent Association, or take in

Wonderful Things Are Happening!

washing in Timbuktu — all I ask is that your plan for me be in operation," when a friend of mine dropped in. She was worried and fearful. She had all the symptoms of cancer, and though she had done a lot of praying in Christian Science, the condition had grown steadily worse. I asked her what she was rebellious about, unhappy about, disturbed about? She admitted she was all three things, because her husband just sat watching television and did nothing. Upon questioning her, I learned that for many years her husband had handled a business successfully for her and her family. Finally he had sold it for them at a profit. Now he wanted to do what he wanted to do. He wanted to move to California, and build a motel and operate it. But this lady did not want to have anything to do with a motel, and she certainly didn't want to move to California. It was a wonderful opportunity to help her see that any wife ought to encourage her husband in his business venture, but especially a Christian Science wife — for all the time she could be knowing it was not what her husband thought was right, or what she thought was right, that would come to pass, but what God knew was right. She could be rejoicing that God's plan for them was in operation, and therefore, wonderful things were happening. I told her the way I had been praying, and I suggested that we put it in her terms, that she didn't care whether she dug gold in Alaska, or lassoed cattle in Argentina, or was a housewife in Indiana, or operated a motel in California, all she wanted was that God's plan be in operation. She promised to pray that way, and she did. The husband built the motel in California. She learned that a business she thought would be boring, was very interesting. One she thought she'd be ashamed of, she was really proud of. She came to appreciate California as a place to live, far more than Indiana. One reason she hadn't wanted to move away from Indiana, was that her son was going into the Navy. She felt that she ought to maintain his home for him there, so that whenever he would have a leave, he could come home. Well, he did join the Navy; he was stationed in California, and was able to

Wonderful Things Are Happening!

come home almost every weekend. And so, from every point of view, it was a complete demonstration.

Oh yes, I must mention the fact that the relationship between the husband and wife was far more wonderful than it had ever been. Naturally, with all the bitterness gone, she was completely healed of cancer. When she wrote to me telling me of her final healing, she expressed gratitude for my sharing this way of praying with her. In the letter, she enclosed the picture of a rock. The rock was the marker of a very early settlement in California, just three miles from their motel. And the name on the rock was Timbuktu. She said, "You see, I have come to Timbuktu after all."

Even though you are completely satisfied with your present situation, even though you might feel that there is nothing left to be desired, I sincerely hope that you will never let a day go by but what you rejoice in the great truth that God's plan for you is in operation, and that there is no other power or presence that can interfere with it. That's the way we can say with absolute certainty that wonderful things are taking place now, and ever will continue to take place.

The Importance of Joy

Several times, you have already heard me say that "I am not concerned about anything, wonderful things are happening," is a positive, joyous attitude. I would like to discuss with you the importance of the qualities of positiveness and joy, in our application of Christian Science. You know, we are not actually practicing Christian Science unless joy is present in our thinking. What would your answer be if I were to ask you, "Are you supremely happy?" In every instance, every single individual in this audience should be able to say without reservation, "Yes, I am supremely happy." Aren't we all followers of Jesus, the Christ? Do we not seek to obey his every command? Jesus saw the importance of joy and gladness,

Wonderful Things Are Happening!

and he was forever telling his followers to rejoice and be exceeding glad, and as a very special message, to which he added, "No man can take your joy from you. These things have I spoken unto you, that my joy might remain in you, and that your joy might be full." You see, Jesus wasn't satisfied with our being a little bit happy, he wanted us to be supremely happy. He wanted our joy to be full. Mrs. Eddy recognized the importance of happiness where she writes in the textbook: "Happiness is spiritual, born of Truth and Love. It is unselfish; therefore it cannot exist alone, but requires all mankind to share it." The Psalms are full of commands to rejoice. "Be glad in the Lord, and rejoice, ye righteous: and shout for joy, all ye that are upright in heart." " . . . thy God, hath anointed thee with the oil of gladness." " . . . yea, happy is that people, whose God is the Lord." Do not these words and the spirit they impart, cause your hearts to be uplifted and make you want to sing praises unto God?

Occasionally you will hear someone say, "I want to be happy, but I don't know *how* to be. How *can* I rejoice when I really am low in spirit, and don't actually feel glad?" Let us deal with happiness, just as we would any other desirable quality. If you want health or wealth, you claim it in its spiritual sense. Therefore, claim happiness now. Not just in a degree, but fully and completely! After all, because we reflect the Supreme Being, we must claim His qualities in the superlative. Claim you are supremely happy. Claim that you are one of the happiest of all the people in the universe. In *Christian Healing*, Mrs. Eddy writes, "If you wish to be happy, argue with yourself on the side of happiness; take the side you wish to carry, and be careful not to talk on both sides, or to argue stronger for sorrow than for joy. You are the attorney for the case, and will win or lose according to your plea."

Just think, Mrs. Eddy has specifically appointed you to be the attorney to plead the case for happiness and joy. Just how have you been pleading the case? Have you been arguing the case for sadness, for moderate joy, or for supreme happiness? Have you

Wonderful Things Are Happening!

been testifying that you are supremely happy *now*, or that you *would be* if something happened, or when some circumstance might be changed? Oh, let us ever win in demonstrating supreme joy by such consistent argument as, "I am supremely happy; I know it; I understand it; I acknowledge it; I am grateful and thrilled to be the happy child of God; not only am I supremely happy, but I feel it. I am demonstrating supreme happiness. In fact, I shout my joy and gladness from the housetops. Moreover, everyone sees me as a supremely happy image and likeness of God." Anyone who testifies concerning his joy in such a manner, cannot help but feel the boundless bliss of Soul and the rapture of divine Mind.

We are claiming only that which is *true* about ourselves. The lie is that man could be capable of being unhappy. Man never having been born into matter, living in the heaven of divine consciousness, sees nothing, hears nothing, feels nothing to be unhappy about. Since he is ever in the presence of God, good, there is only one cause for joy and rapture in his experience. Mrs. Eddy established the fact that man is ever at the standpoint of joy when she writes in the textbook: "Man is not a pendulum, swinging between . . . joy and sorrow." Notice how Mrs. Eddy puts no limitation on the joy that we are to express, for she emphasizes that man is tributary to boundless bliss.

It is much easier to demonstrate happiness if our cause for happiness is scientific. What is it that makes you happy? Is it person, place, or thing? Is it home, church, or employment? Is it human events or circumstances? Are you ever tempted to say, "I shall be happy when. . ." or "I would be happy if. . . ." There is only one sure, safe, permanent basis for happiness, and that is *God*. Over and over, the Bible tells us to rejoice in the Lord. Our textbook tells us, "Happiness would be more readily attained and would be more secure in our keeping, if sought in Soul." "Rejoice and be exceeding glad" that it is God that makes you happy. I know that many of you have heard the beautiful solo sung in our churches which ends with the line, "God is — this is enough to know."

Wonderful Things Are Happening!

Plead the case for happiness with absolute conviction that just the existence of God is enough to produce joy and happiness. Whenever I find myself tempted to express anything other than joy, I open our textbook to these lines: "Unfathomable Mind is expressed. The depth, breadth, height, might, majesty, and glory of infinite Love fill all space. That is enough!" It is truly thrilling to contemplate the depth of Love, the breadth of Love, the height of Love, the might of Love, the majesty of Love, and the glory of infinite Love filling all space. And then I ask myself, "Is that enough to make you supremely happy?" Then I have to admit, "It certainly is!"

Oh, isn't it wonderful that our happiness cannot be limited or restricted by human circumstances? Our joy does not depend upon whether or not we can buy that automobile, or get that apartment, or marry that girl, or win that election, or receive that inheritance, or obtain that salary increase, or experience that healing. No, our happiness depends solely upon the fact that *God is*. Therefore, our joy and happiness can never be taken from us, for God, our one and only cause for happiness, is forever with us.

How often do we say, "I'll be happy when this event takes place," or "I'll be happy if the circumstances change." This is actually postponing our happiness, or our heaven. Such an attitude can be compared to an individual who would take a car that was smoking hot, smelled funny, made funny noises, into a filling station, and then when the attendant would tell him that he needed oil, he would respond, "When my car runs smoothly, when it no longer gets hot and makes any unpleasant noise, then I will reward it with a quart of oil." How foolish! The oil must go in first, then the car will run smoothly. Just so in our daily experience. We must first pour in the oil of gladness; then our human affairs will be lubricated so as to run smoothly.

It really makes no difference what your profession — you will be a better teacher, lawyer, carpenter, office manager, accountant, housewife, businessman, if you are rejoicing in the Lord. Our

Wonderful Things Are Happening!

work is done more quickly, more effortlessly, more successfully, when we are serving with joy and gladness. It is much easier to demonstrate the right sense of home, companionship, supply, employment, harmonious relationships with others, if we claim the joy that is ours.

Not only is it true that pouring in the oil of gladness benefits all of our affairs, but it benefits our bodies, our health. If we wish to be healthy, we should take great doses of the oil of gladness. There is absolutely no better medicine. Way back in the days of Solomon, Solomon himself recognized that man's health was influenced by his thinking. Solomon pleaded the case against unhappiness and for joy when he said, "A merry heart doeth good like a medicine: but a broken spirit drieth the bones."

Did you ever hear of a supremely happy individual manifesting heart trouble, skin disease, arthritis, rheumatism, digestive difficulties, tuberculosis, or cancer? No, none of these claims can be manifested when supreme happiness, on the basis of God's allness, is being consistently manifested. In fact, no matter what the physical claim may be, one of the most important steps in annihilating the error is to help the patient find his true happiness. Joy and gladness heal. Remember that Jesus asked the palsied man to rejoice before he was healed. He said, "Son, be of good cheer; thy sins be forgiven thee."

A second Reader in one of our churches in my home city suddenly found herself unable to walk. The condition proved embarrassing to her as well as alarming, because here it was the end of the week, she was supposed to read Sunday, and introduce a lecturer Monday night. It seemed that the harder she worked in Science, the worse became her condition. Finally, she stopped working. She turned to God and said, "Father, if I never walk again, I know that You are my loving Father-Mother God, and I am Your image and likeness." She said, in giving her testimony, that she was so happy, so thrilled, so blissful in the knowledge that God was her

WONDERFUL THINGS ARE HAPPENING!

Father-Mother, that she honestly didn't care if she ever walked again. It was then that she was healed. She was so thrilled, so happy, so satisfied, so contented that God was her Father-Mother, that absolutely nothing else was important — not even walking. No wonder she had her healing! She was literally putting God first, and the walking was added unto her.

Do you remember that in the opening testimony I brought out a couple of times that, regardless of what came up in the bodies or in the affairs of these individuals, they refused to be concerned, and they rejoiced that wonderful things were taking place? I am asking all of you today to adopt that same joyous approach to things. Regardless of what appears to take place in your bodies or in your affairs, maintain your joy, argue and plead for the case of happiness, demonstrate boundless bliss — on the basis that God is the source of your joy and happiness, and therefore it can never be taken from you. Then you, too, will be seeing wonderful things take place.

The Positive Attitude

How would you rate yourself as a Christian Scientist — positive or negative? Remember that in the testimony given, it was the positive attitude, as well as the joyous attitude, which brought about such wonderful results. Do you accept the truth wholeheartedly, without any reservation? If you do, then you are positive. If error seems to present itself, do you instantly reverse it and substitute the truth? If so, you are positive. Are you absolutely sure and certain that God is All, and everything is perfect? Rate yourself positive. Are you constant, consistent, unwavering, steadfast, and even stubborn in standing with the Truth? If so, rate yourself A plus for positiveness. What about your expectation? Are you always expecting wonderful things to happen? Do you have absolute faith that only good can come to pass? If so, this is evidence that you are positive.

WONDERFUL THINGS ARE HAPPENING!

Here are some bits of evidence which point to negative Christian Scientists. The individual *hopes* that he can be healed, rather than *knowing* that he will be; the one who thinks that Christian Science works for everybody else, but not for him; and the individual who is always expecting that the worst will happen. Then you've heard of this attitude, "It is just too good to be true." And what about such comments as, "Oh yes, I know I'm really perfect, but I certainly don't manifest it." Or, "I have a rich heavenly Father, but He hasn't shared any of His wealth with me."

Then there's the individual who is sure one minute, and not so sure the next; standing steadfast in the truth one day, but wavering the next; resolving never to give up the perfect concept, and then giving it up at the very first presentation of error. Oh, aren't you glad that none of these descriptions, that might apply to a negative Christian Scientist, fits you? Listen to what the dictionary has to say about the word *positive* and you will see that it is a qualification which is essential to being a Christian Scientist: "Confident, certain, sure." And I loved this added bit: "Aggressively certain."

In knowing that God is All, and that He is expressing Himself, and therefore the results have to be wonderful, how much more thrilling it is to be confident, certain, sure, rather than to lack confidence, to be uncertain or unsure. Another definition is, "Leaving no doubt." There certainly isn't any doubt as to the outcome of an individual's experience when you hear him say, "I'm not concerned about anything, wonderful things are taking place." In our own thinking, in our own contemplation, in our own praying, there should never be any doubt about the allness of God and the perfection of His creation. There should only be absolute conviction that God is All, and everything is perfect. And oh, how important it is in the sharing of our thinking with others, that our every statement carries a ring of sureness, confidence, conviction that good is supreme, and therefore God's blessings are ever at hand.

What kind of God do you have? Is there any interruption in His being All-in-all? Is there ever any uncertainty in God as

Wonderful Things Are Happening!

Principle, any deviation in God as Truth, any inconsistency in God as Love? James gives us a wonderful description of our positive, changeless God when he writes, "Every good gift and every perfect gift is from above, and cometh down from the Father of lights, with whom is no variableness, neither shadow of turning." Thus, because we are the children of God, made in His image and likeness, we have no choice but to express the qualities of "no variableness, neither shadow of turning."

We are all familiar with that glorious promise of freedom, if we will but know the truth; but there is a certain prerequisite given in knowing the truth. When Jesus said, " . . . ye shall know the truth, and the truth shall make you free," the prerequisite he presented was, "If ye continue in my word, — ye shall know the truth, and the truth shall make you free."

When is it that we are most aware of the presence of God? When is it that we feel His presence, see His allness, behold His perfect universe and His perfect man? Is it not when we continue in His word? Is it not when we "hold thought steadfastly to the enduring, the good, and the true"? In *Science and Health*, Mrs. Eddy tells us, "Hold thought steadfastly to the enduring, the good, and the true, and you will bring these into your experience proportionably to their occupancy of your thoughts." Oh, then is when the inspiration of divine Mind pours into our waiting consciousness. Then is when we are filled with "the knowledge of the Lord, as the waters cover the sea." Do you remember Stephen's experience? It was when Stephen looked steadfastly into heaven that he "saw the glory of God, and Jesus standing on the right hand of God."

The attitude of steadfastness is essential to healing. Our Leader gives a special rule for healing when she states, "When the illusion of sickness or sin tempts you, cling steadfastly to God and His idea. Allow nothing but His likeness to abide in your thought. Let neither fear nor doubt overshadow your clear sense and calm

Wonderful Things Are Happening!

trust, that the recognition of life harmonious — as Life eternally is — can destroy any painful sense of, or belief in, that which Life is not."

The attitude of dominion, of standing steadfast, of persistence, of constancy, of immovableness, is a demand made upon us by our heavenly Father. It is a law laid upon us by Christian Science. Therefore, we have no choice but to be steadfast and constant. However, this is not beyond our ability. Dominion is our heritage. We inherit the dominion to be constant and steadfast from our heavenly Father, with whom there is no variableness. Moreover, God knowingly gave man dominion over all. In speaking of this dominion, our Leader says, "His birthright is dominion, not subjection. He is lord of the belief in earth and heaven, — himself subordinate alone to his Maker. This is the Science of being." (*Science and Health*)

Controlled by Truth, we are forced to manifest consistence and invariableness. And with God as our Mind, governing and controlling us, we have no choice but to be sure and positive. Mrs. Eddy tells us to hold perpetually this thought that "it is the spiritual idea, the Holy Ghost and Christ, which enables you to demonstrate, with scientific certainty." This makes it very clear that we are not alone in our efforts to express dominion. God is ever at hand, not only enabling us, but impelling us, compelling us, forcing us to demonstrate with certainty, with sureness, with positiveness, with constancy, with persistence, the rules of healing. Notice that in presenting this statement, Mrs. Eddy does not say that we should have this thought today, but not tomorrow; or that we should have the thought every other hour. She says, "Hold perpetually this thought." Oh, there is certainly no variableness or deviation in her approach, is there?

There is a little prayer that Mrs. Eddy once shared with a student of hers that has enabled me to express my dominion in standing steadfast. This is a prayer she gave to Laura Lathrop, when she asked her to establish Second Church in New York City. "There is no other mind to tempt me, harm me, or control me. I spiritually understand this, and am master of the occasion." It is because of the one infinite Mind controlling us that we are incapable of being weak or lacking in confidence, steadfastness and constancy. We cannot even be tempted to lose faith or to be uncertain. Instead, we are master of the occasion. We are those steadfast, positive, sure, certain, consistent, persistent children of that one Father-Mother God "with whom there is no variableness, neither shadow of turning."

I would like to conclude this discussion on the importance of positiveness with Paul's words: "Therefore, my beloved brethren, be ye stedfast, unmoveable, always abounding in the work of the Lord, forasmuch as ye know that your labour is not in vain in the Lord."

ABOUT THE AUTHOR: Dorothy Rieke was a Christian Science practitioner, and the wife of Herbert E. Rieke, a highly respected Christian Science teacher and lecturer. They lived in Indianapolis, Indiana. Mrs. Rieke supported her husband in his work, accompanying him on world-wide lecture tours. After his passing, she continued in the healing work. She also wrote and delivered two outstanding association addresses — *Wonderful Things Are Happening* and *Immortality Brought to Light*. Copies of these addresses were quietly circulated throughout the Christian Science Field for many years, before they were published as booklets. Mrs. Rieke passed on in 1996.

For further information on Christian Science:
  Write   The Bookmark
          Post Office Box 801143
          Santa Clarita, CA 91380
  Call   1-800-220-7767
  Visit our website: www.thebookmark.com

Mpengo of the Congo

by Grace W. McGavran

Illustrated by Kurt Wiese

Cover design by Phillip Colhouer
Cover illustration by Larissa Sharina
First published in 1945
This unabridged version has updated grammar and spelling.
© 2019 Jenny Phillips
goodandbeautiful.com

Table of Contents

Foreword 1

Mpengo Goes A-Fishing 5

News of Hidden Village 12

On the Great Luapa River 17

More About Hidden Village 22

First Days in Hidden Village 27

School in Hidden Village 33

The Blessing of the Gardens 38

Learning the Village Ways 44

When Little New One Came 50

A Visit from the Missionary 57

Big-Fish-Catching Day 64

The Broken Leg 68

The Journey to the Mission 74

At the Mission Station 81

At Home in Hidden Village 87

Foreword

△·△·△·△·△
▽·▽·▽·▽·▽

Across the sea from America, toward the rising sun, lies the great continent of Africa.

Ships carry precious cargo of its products to all the world. Airplanes skim over its forests and deserts, its fertile fields and mountains. Buses run across its deserts.

Its people are mostly dark-skinned with black eyes and black hair. But some who live there have brown skin, and a few have white.

Down through Central Africa to the western coast rolls the mighty Congo River. Steamers move up and down its waters. Many big rivers empty into it.

Great forests grow beside the river. The country all around it is called the Congo. The people live in villages in the forests.

The story you are going to read is about a little boy named Mpengo and his sister, Ekila, who live in the

Congo country. Their mother and father live there, too. So do all their people.

Missionaries have gone to that hot forest land. For many, many years they have worked and taught there.

Mpengo's grandparents on his father's side are Christians. Mpengo's mother and father are Christians. They all live in a mission village. But the father of Mpengo's mother lives in a faraway village. He will not listen to the Christian teaching. He is a witch doctor.

And because of the faraway village and the witch doctor grandfather, adventures came to Mpengo and Ekila.

All over Central Africa, inside and outside the Congo country, there are villages like those Mpengo knew. In some of them, the story of Jesus has never been heard. Each year the missionaries are taking the story of Jesus into more villages. The native preachers and teachers are helping, just as Mpengo's father did.

*To Anne and Alison
who were the very first
to hear this story*

Mpengo looked down into the pit.

1

MPENGO GOES A-FISHING

Mpengo skipped merrily through the bushes, keeping out of sight of anyone passing. He was running away from school. Not that he disliked school. Of all the boys who had come from up and down the great Congo River to the mission school, Mpengo liked school the best. Of all the boys in the third year of school, he liked it the best.

But today was different.

In one hand Mpengo had a fishing pole. In the other he held a gleaming American fishhook. It had been brought to him all the way from the great city of Chicago by his special friend Tommy White.

Tommy had arrived back in Africa from that faraway place just the day before. He had brought Mpengo the fishhook for a present.

Mpengo simply could not wait until school was out to try that fishhook. Tommy had fixed a pole with a line, a bobber, a sinker, and the hook in true American style. Mpengo was sure he could catch a huge fish. So he went very quietly toward the river. He came to the steep bank of the quick-flowing Luapa River, not far above where it joined the huge, dark Congo River. "Here," he thought, "will be a good place to fish."

Mpengo crept down the bank. There were people on the beach who might send him back to school. He squeezed through a hole in the bushes. He got ready to fish. Lying on the bank off at one side was what looked like a log. In the other direction, a bush was between him and the open part of the beach. Mpengo grinned with delight. His black eyes danced as he thought, "What a very cozy hideout!" No one would notice his dark brown skin, even if they looked in that direction. If he scooped a little hole in the sand and sat there quietly, no one could catch a glimpse of his dark blue shorts.

Mpengo's bobber was soon floating quietly in the backwater. He glanced over at the log which was covered with weeds. Under the weeds he saw an eye open and stare at him. Mpengo shivered from head to foot.

"Ae-oh!" muttered Mpengo. "It's no log at all. No log at all! Why didn't I think about Old Crocodile? *Now* what shall I do?"

The eye opened again. Mpengo gathered his feet under him, crouching, but he did not try to stand up. Instead, he moved one foot after the other very slowly. He never took his eye from that of Old Crocodile. He could see the long, cruel snout lying flat to the ground and the enormous tail that could swing in a flash and knock a small boy into the river.

Mpengo moved an inch at a time toward the bush. If he could just get around behind it, he could leap to his feet and run.

Old Crocodile moved a little. Mpengo dared not hurry. He inched along hoping that Old Crocodile would be fooled.

There was a loud shout. Someone grabbed Mpengo by the shoulders and lifted him right over the bush and out of reach of that fearful tail. Old Crocodile slipped into the brown waters so quietly that you would never have thought he had ever dreamed of having Small Boy for supper.

But Mpengo was very frightened at being grabbed

*He never took his eye from that of
Old Crocodile.*

from behind. He struggled and yelled and waved his fishing pole wildly. Up came the bobber, the sinker, and the hook. And just as Big Inkema set that small boy down all ready to scold him for starting to fish where Old Crocodile was sunning himself, he felt the fishhook bite into his shoulder and fasten itself firmly under his skin.

Big Inkema's words were very angry as he twisted and turned and tried to get the fishhook out. Mpengo covered his mouth with his hand and watched in horror. He had caught his fishhook into Big Inkema, who had saved his life! But when he offered to try to get it out, Inkema only scowled.

"It will have to be cut out!" he muttered. Then he shouted suddenly, "Ai!"

For Mpengo had given a little jerk without meaning to, and the fishhook had bitten deeper into Big Inkema's shoulder.

Eight-year-old Mpengo felt very, very small as he stood there with Big Inkema glaring down at him. He gulped and blinked. "I did not mean to! Truly, Inkema, I am sorry."

Big Inkema took the pole and held it so that the line did not pull. He did not scowl any more, but neither did he smile. Why should he, with a fishhook caught in his shoulder? He looked very stern. All the little scars where his face had been marked in a tribal design when he was a tiny boy stood out.

Mpengo looked at those scars. They made good-natured Big Inkema look very fierce. "I'm glad Big Inkema isn't *really* fierce," thought Mpengo.

"Come," said Big Inkema. "We will go to the mission hospital. Tommy's father can cut the hook out." He looked down at Mpengo. "Better come along and get your pole and line." He chuckled suddenly and added, "After this big fish is unhooked from the end of it!"

Mpengo followed Big Inkema anxiously up the steep bank. He trotted along the path under the palm trees, trying hard to keep up. What would Dr. White, who was Tommy's father, say? He was so very busy after having been away for a whole year. He would not be pleased at having to attend to a business like this!

But Dr. White was too busy even to be cross. In a flash he was at work. Mpengo stood on one foot watching while the fishhook was taken out. Nurse Eoto held it up.

"Whose is the fishhook?" she asked as she looked closely at it.

"It *was* mine," said Mpengo in a small, sorry voice. "But now it is Inkema's to tell him I am sorry and to say thank you for saving me from the crocodile." He looked hopefully at Inkema. He did not like to have Inkema cross at him.

Inkema took the hook and grunted. Then he looked at it closely. "It is the hook Tommy gave you? No?" he inquired.

Mpengo nodded.

Inkema admired it. Then he handed it back. There was a broad smile on his face. "It was an accident. You must not give away the gift that was brought for you. It is enough that you wanted to give it. Besides," he teased, "you will need it where you are going."

"Where is that?" asked Mpengo.

But Big Inkema would not tell. "Go away!" he said. "It is time for me to get to work."

Big Inkema turned to go into the hospital ward. He was learning to be a nurse. Dr. White was training him and other fine, strong young men. When they had learned to do a nurse's work, and when they knew something about medicines, they could go far away into the deep forest and help the village people living there.

Every boy in Mpengo's school hoped that Big Inkema would be a nurse in *his* village. Every boy and girl loved Big Inkema with his scarred-up face and his jolly smile.

Inkema winked at Mpengo. But he said never a word more about where Mpengo would be going.

2

News of Hidden Village

Mpengo could not get anyone to say anything more about the trip Inkema had talked about.

"Ask your father. Ask your mother," said Nurse Eoto. "Shall a person outside of the family tell you the news? But this one thing I will say: All the people of the church are proud of what your father plans to do."

Mpengo hurried down the path by the banana trees toward his own house with its neat brick walls and its thatch of palm leaves. He could not wait to find out what it was that his father was going to do. Something of which the whole church was proud! He broke into a fast trot.

His mother was busy fixing the supper.

His mother, Nganda, was busy fixing the greens for supper. She looked at Mpengo, her face wrinkling into a thousand happy crinkles. She smiled at his eager question and patted his shoulder. "Where are we going? Ai, what a question! Who said we were going anywhere?"

"Inkema said—" Mpengo burst out.

"Well, and he said true. But your father wished to tell you and your sister Ekila with his own lips when he came back from the trip on the river."

"But he will not be back until tomorrow. I cannot wait. Most truly, my Mother, I cannot wait."

"Then I will tell it. Listen, Mpengo, and listen well. Far up the mighty Luapa River and away up one of its branches, there is a place called Hidden Village. It is the village where I, your mother, lived when a small girl. There lives your uncle, Tula, and your grandfather, Tulagi, the witch doctor. The village men are hunters, and the womenfolk plant gardens in patches cleared out from the forest. Wild animals are many. The people of the village live in fear of the witch doctor and his charms. There is no school and no church. It is there that we are going—your father and I, you and your sister Ekila, and Baby Bula."

Mpengo stared at her. "But why?"

His mother stirred the greens in the smooth earthen pot she herself had made. She had molded it very carefully from clay and baked it in a hot oven until it was shiny and strong. The smoke from the fire beneath drifted into their faces.

"Because," she said, "three families in that village came here many months ago and heard the story of Jesus and His message that God loves them. They listened to the teaching with all their hearts. They became followers of Jesus."

"But why—" Mpengo interrupted.

"Wait! Have patience! It is too long a story for short telling." His mother knelt and blew the fire until it leaped up around the sides of the pot. "The three Christian families have asked for a teacher. Their chief has asked for one, too. So our church has said that it will send a Christian family to live in that faraway village and help the people there. We are the family."

Mpengo looked sober for a minute. Then he gave a wild yell and leaped and danced. "I will catch an elephant! I will become a great hunter!" he shouted. "Hi-yi! I will go and get old Begalo to make me a spear."

His mother laughed again. "Go, then, mighty hunter! But in the meantime—" She stopped short. "Why, small imp, are you not in school?" she asked severely.

Before Mpengo had time to answer, Ekila came hurrying home from school. She was only seven years old while Mpengo was eight. Sometimes he felt a great deal older than Ekila. But her black eyes were always ready to dance with fun when he suggested something to do. She was always ready to run errands. She could cook small meals between the regular ones her mother prepared. To a hungry boy like Mpengo, that was wonderful. Ekila was at the top of her class, too. Mpengo was proud of his little sister who knew more than the little brothers of the other boys.

So now he burst into talk, telling her all he knew and all he could guess about the journey they were to take.

"I will get Begalo to make you a spear, too," he offered.

But his mother spoke quickly. "No, no, Mpengo! Girls do not use spears." Then she started to say something else and stopped.

"What words were you going to say?" asked Ekila.

"Words you will not like. In Hidden Village the boys play with the boys and the girls with the girls. It is not so in this Christian place where we live."

Ekila and Mpengo looked at each other. "What a strange rule," they thought.

"But you will find friends. Both of you! Of that I am sure." Mother Nganda dished out the greens. "Time to eat," she said.

3

On the Great Luapa River

Darkness filled the house of Mpengo. But in the darkness his father, Iso Thomas, stirred. A sleepy bird had chirped in the forest.

"Time to get up," said Iso Thomas.

Mpengo rolled slowly off his sleeping mat. Suddenly he was wide awake. Was it really to happen today?

His father lit the lantern. Mpengo looked around. Yes, the bundles were ready, and his mother, Nganda, was rolling and tying her sleeping mat. Today was the day! Mpengo leaped to his feet. Today! Today! Today they were starting on the long journey upriver to the village hidden in the dark, dark forest.

It didn't take long to prepare some food to be eaten

Mpengo rolled slowly off his sleeping mat.

in the mid-morning on the boat. Ekila was given the food to carry.

Just as it became light, some of the church people arrived to help take the family belongings down to the mission steamer. Mpengo carried his fishing pole. This time its hook was neatly fastened so that it could not catch on anyone's skin. Ekila carried her baby brother tied to her back.

As they went down the path to the river beach, the sun came up. Everywhere the people of the church could be seen hurrying along the pathways down to the beach. They were coming to see Iso Thomas and his family off and send them to Hidden Village with a blessing.

Mpengo danced ahead to the sandy beach. Tommy White and the boys from school were already there, all chattering as noisily as monkeys in the trees. The mission steamer looked very small in the great flowing river.

Captain John waved to Mpengo and the other boys. He was busy getting the boat ready to start. The men who helped to run the boat were hard at work.

Iso Thomas and some of the men of the church carried the bundles up the gangplank. Mpengo and his friends skipped up it merrily. Ekila was a bit afraid of walking along that narrow wooden road between the shore and the boat. She handed Baby Bula over to her mother to carry. Soon the family was all on board.

Then they were ready to start. The friends from the mission went on shore.

Mark Mpoku, the pastor, was standing on the shore with the church people. He prayed a prayer of blessing on the travelers. Everyone sang a hymn.

The rope that tied the steamer to the shore was unfastened. The paddle wheels started to turn.

Soon the steamer was around the bend, and Mpengo and Ekila saw nothing but river and forest around them.

All day long the steamer pushed against the current on its way upstream. Sometimes it passed canoes, made of hollowed-out logs, so big that it took many men to paddle them. The men shouted greetings. Sometimes Captain John found it hard not to hit a sand bar. Once, a huge uprooted tree nearly struck the paddle wheel. In the afternoon the steamer passed a village on the bank. Captain John took the boat up to the beach so that passengers might get on and off.

When evening came, Captain John brought the steamer into a little harbor, which was just a sandy beach in a curve of the river. Great piles of firewood were gathered on the shore. The boatmen tied up the boat. Iso Thomas and the men went up to the village, which was in the forest back from the river bank. Captain John bought some of the wood from the village men. The boatmen carried it on board. The steamer could not run without wood to burn in its engine.

Ekila and her mother built a little fire on the beach and cooked a good meal for the family. Baby Bula toddled around, glad to be on the ground again.

Then darkness came.

After the evening meal, the village people came down to the beach. They sat around the fire that Captain John had built upon the shore and talked. Captain John preached to them. He and the boatmen and Iso Thomas and the other Christians among the passengers sang about God's love and greatness and goodness. Mpengo and Ekila went to sleep, all tired out. They never knew when Captain John and Iso Thomas carried them back onto the steamer and laid them down on their sleeping mats on the deck.

4

More About Hidden Village

When Mpengo and Ekila woke up the next morning, the paddle wheels were churning. The day's journey had started.

Iso Thomas and Captain John were talking.

"Yes," Iso Thomas was saying, "Swahini, the chief of Hidden Village, asked for a teacher to come to the village. But Tula, the brother of my wife, is very angry about it."

"No wonder!" said Captain John. "Tula's father, you told me, is the witch doctor. When he dies, Tula will be the village witch doctor. If the people become Christians, he will have no power over them. I can see why he is not happy about your coming."

"Tula is a fine fellow," said Iso Thomas. "There is nothing that would please me more than for him to become a Christian. He is the sort of man that other people follow, wherever he leads. He would make a fine Christian leader."

Mpengo was glad to hear that Uncle Tula was a fine fellow. And he didn't worry in the least about Grandfather being a witch doctor. His father turned to him and to Ekila.

"They are going to build a house for us, just like the other houses in Hidden Village," said Iso Thomas. "We are going to try to keep it clean, in a village where other houses are not clean. We will keep the ground around it clear and neat. We shall have happiness and love and laughter and kindness in our house. That way the village people can see the Christian way of living."

Sitting on the deck, Mpengo hung his feet over the edge of the boat. Ekila sat beside him. They liked to see the water slipping by beneath their feet. They held to the railing, for they did not want to fall into the river where Old Crocodile's relatives lived. Ekila and Mpengo sat very quietly, listening to the talk of the men. Some of it they could not understand. But some they could.

Neither Ekila nor Mpengo had ever lived in a place where people did not know about Christian ways.

"I wonder if I shall like it," whispered Mpengo. But soon he was thinking about the plans he had made for hunting. Perhaps Uncle Tula would take him hunting. He wriggled with excitement at the thought.

About noon the steamer came to the place where a small stream emptied into the big river.

"Here," said Captain John, "we turn and go back."

"But what about us?" Mpengo asked him.

"You will go in a dugout canoe to the fork of the small river," said Captain John. "And from the fork of the stream you will go by trail, walking through the forest."

Soon Mpengo's family was all tucked into the dugout canoe that had been sent to meet them. With a shout, the men who had come from Hidden Village dipped their paddles into the water. Slowly the big, clumsy canoe started up against the current.

It was night when the family reached the fork of the stream. From there they would have to go on by foot the next day. The village at the fork of the stream was friendly. They would stay in it for the night.

Ekila did not like it. For one thing, the hut where they slept was not clean. For another, she was afraid of the men with spears and shields who came and went in the village. Even their new friends who had paddled the canoe carried weapons and looked very fierce.

Slowly the canoe started up against the current.

"Why do they carry spears?" she whispered to her mother.

"Because these people are not Christians, even though they are friendly to us. And where the villages are not Christian, the people fear their neighbors in other villages," said her mother. "When the men from different tribes become Christian, they are not afraid of each other. Then the spears rest inside the houses, and the shields lean idly against the walls. The people of a village do not make war against the villages of other tribes then."

"Will there be spears and shields in our village?" asked Ekila.

"There will be spears and shields," said her mother, "because the people of the villages around are not Christian. So they are not always friendly."

"Mpengo is wanting a spear," said Ekila, doubtfully.

"For hunting," said her mother. "It was of spears for fighting that we were talking. The men need them to hunt animals for food, of course. We womenfolk plant and care for the gardens and cook the meat of the animals the men kill."

5

First Days in Hidden Village

Early the next morning the men from Hidden Village who had paddled the canoe were ready to start. They loaded the bundles that belonged to Iso Thomas and his family onto their heads and shoulders. The whole family set out along the dark forest trail.

Great trees made deep shadows over the trail. It was like a dim tunnel through the forest. As they moved along, monkeys jumped through the trees near them, chattering and scolding in the branches. They went slowly and stopped often to rest. Mother Nganda was carrying the heavy baby. She and the children got very tired after several hours of walking.

*Monkeys chattered and scolded
in the branches.*

First Days in Hidden Village

It was late in the afternoon when they reached Hidden Village where Chief Swahini greeted them. They saw the untidy houses straggling down both sides of the path. A little way apart from the rest was a new house. Its frame was of heavy poles. Its sides were clay walls. Its roof was a thatch of palm leaves. It was just like all the other houses of the village except that it was new. Because it was new, it was clean. There the family belongings were put.

Mpengo, keeping very close to his father's heels, followed him to the place where Chief Swahini and the men were waiting to talk. Near Swahini was a boy just Mpengo's own age.

It was Mato, the son of the chief. He grinned at Mpengo. Mpengo smiled back. And with that they were friends. Mato was taller, but Mpengo thought he could get him down in a wrestling match. He wondered, while the men talked, whether Mato would enjoy a friendly tussle. He didn't notice the angry-looking man who was Uncle Tula.

Back at the new house, Mother Nganda and Ekila were very busy with women's work. Nganda began housekeeping right away. She put the sleeping mats where they would be easy to find. Ekila went with Kamili, one of the village girls, to get water from the little stream. Before very long Nganda had a fire burning around the sides of the big black clay pot in which food for supper was cooking.

Mpengo and his father came to the house when it was time to eat. Mother Nganda looked at her husband. There was a question in her eyes.

"Your brother, Tula, is very angry. He says he will have the witch doctor make a charm against us," said Iso.

Ekila held her breath. "A charm against us!" she thought, and a little shiver went over her. She had heard new girls at school tell about horrible things that the witch doctors could do.

But her mother only laughed softly. "The charms of the witch doctor are nothing but feather and bone and a few words. They cannot hurt us," she said. "Why should Tula be so angry?"

"He has heard that Christian men help start new gardens, which he says is women's work. He says we will change all the old ways and spoil the village," said Iso. "It is quite true we hope to persuade our people to give up old ways that are not good. But there are many old ways that *are* good. Christian people will always want to keep the good ways."

"I saw Uncle Tula putting up a strange something by the pathway," said Mpengo. "I was in the bushes."

"What did it look like?" asked his father.

"Just a bunch of old feathers and stuff," said Mpengo.

His father looked at him thoughtfully. "Uncle Tula was probably putting up a fetish," he said. "That is something over which a witch doctor has said a magic charm. Most of the people here think the forest is full of evil spirits. They think a fetish will keep the spirits from harming them. They are full of fear. We, who are Christians, know they are mistaken. We are going to try to help the people to learn that there is nothing to be afraid of. We are going to help them to know that God is their loving Father."

From the very first day, Mpengo liked living in the village. He found that everyone was friendly. Because of the shining hook and line, all the village boys were eager to take him fishing. Mpengo let each one fish with the hook. They did everything they could to show Mpengo the ways of living in the forest.

Early one morning Mato offered to show Mpengo the elephant pit. By starting early the boys could be back in time for the school that Iso Thomas had already started. Mato did not want to miss a single lesson. But it was rather dull for Mpengo because Iso was at first too busy to give him third-grade lessons.

Mato led the way along a path. He took Mpengo out

beyond the gardens. They came upon a deep pit dug right across the path. It was covered with branches and a little earth and dead leaves. "The wild elephants sometimes come and tear up the gardens. The next time they come one of them will fall into the pit. He will be killed, and the rest will go away because they are afraid," said Mato.

Mpengo peered down into the pit through a little hole among the leaves. "It has sharp stakes in it," he said. "If a person fell in, he would be hurt."

"If any person comes without warning," said Mato, "he must expect to be hurt. This is not the travel path to the village. Anyone walking here should be careful."

Mpengo looked around to see just where the pit was. He was not going to fall into it himself by mistake!

Mato looked up through the forest branches toward the sun. "It is the time of learning," he said. "Come, let us go."

6

School in Hidden Village

Iso Thomas was already busy with the small boys of the village when Mato and Mpengo got there. He was beginning to teach them to read. He and Mpengo and the others had made a place on which the children could write. It was a little sand table, right on the ground.

Iso bent over and made letters with his finger in the sand. The children copied them.

Mpengo helped the children to learn. Because he was in the third grade in school, he could help his father teach the boys. Not one of the boys had ever, in all his life, had one single day of school. Mpengo felt very important. But today his father, with a smile in his eyes, gave Mpengo very hard lessons of his own to do. He wanted his son to know that he still had much to learn.

The children learned reading and writing. They learned singing, too. But of all the things that happened in school, they liked two the best. One was to hear stories from the Bible. The other was to learn and sing the Christian songs.

Only the boys were in the school at first. It was hard-work time in the gardens. All the girls had to help their mothers. Ekila had to help, too. She was not very happy when she found out that Mpengo and the boys would be allowed to study while she dug and hoed and gathered and carried. She had to spend a lot of time looking after Baby Bula while her mother worked. The baby was eager to go toddling off into the forest. Besides that, he was just as willing to eat large black ants as anything else his little fingers could pick up from the ground.

"What a nuisance a baby is," sighed Ekila. Then she hugged him until he squirmed his fat little body in her arms and sent up a howl.

Ekila really loved Baby Bula. She kept him washed and clean and sweet. She put him to sleep in his basket-cradle when the time came. She fed him at the proper hours.

The little girls of the village brought their baby

brothers and sisters to the home of Ekila. The ground around the house was clean and smooth. The babies could crawl without getting hurt. As they watched Ekila washing Baby Bula, the girls began to want their own small brothers and sisters to be sweet and clean, too. They began to bring basket-cradles, and the place soon looked like a nursery.

Sometimes Ekila told them stories. Sometimes she taught them the Christian songs. There was happiness around the house of Ekila.

But sometimes Ekila felt sad. She wished she could go to school. She longed to be among the rows of people in church. She missed the friends she had left behind. She was just a little afraid of Uncle Tula's scowl and of the cross looks that some of the village people gave her.

"Never mind," comforted her mother. "What happens when someone does a kind deed, Ekila?"

"It makes happiness," said Ekila.

"And if many people do kind and loving acts?" asked Mother.

"There is more happiness," said Ekila.

"True. Now here is a place where there is much unhappiness and unkindness and fear of the spirits. But around our house is little unhappiness, for we are trying to live like a Christian family. In the houses of the three Christian families, there is more and more happiness.

The babies could crawl without getting hurt.

They are learning to love God and to live in His ways and do loving things. When all the people here live in the Christian way, Hidden Village will be a happy place."

Ekila wrinkled up her forehead. "If we went away, the three Christian families could show them," she said slowly.

But Mother Nganda shook her head.

"Listen!" she said.

From the home of one of the Christian families came a loud noise of quarreling.

"The three families are only just beginning to learn. You and Mpengo need your father and me to teach you how to act in Christian ways. The new Christian families have asked us to help them to learn. Can we go away and leave them without a teacher?"

"No," said Ekila, "we cannot do that. I shall not mind staying."

"You *do* have some happy times here," smiled her mother. "Is it not so?"

"Yes," said Ekila. "We do have happy times. I shall think about the happy times and not about the lonely times."

"Why not teach the girls some of the singing-clapping games you learned at school?" suggested her mother.

"I will! I will! That will be fun!" said Ekila with a happy smile.

7

The Blessing of the Gardens

"Everything would be all right if Uncle Tula did not keep stirring up trouble," grumbled Mpengo.

"I heard him speaking to Chief Swahini," said Ekila, nodding her head wisely. "They were talking about the planting of the gardens."

Iso Thomas looked up from his work. He was making a copy of some Bible verses for the children to read at school. He was using a precious piece of paper he had brought with him. There was no place to buy teaching books in this jungle village. There was no place to buy paper, and there was no blackboard. "Tell me what you heard," said Iso to Ekila.

Ekila felt very important. "I was behind the hut of

the chief," she said, "playing with Kamili. Uncle Tula did not know we were there. He and the chief talked about having a big dance with strong drink and many drums. They said something about making a sacrifice to the spirits so the gardens would grow."

"I will talk to the chief," said Iso Thomas. "Maybe the people are beginning to understand that it is God who has planned seedtime and harvest. Maybe they are ready to ask God's blessing on their gardens. Perhaps they are ready to give up making sacrifices to evil spirits who can do them neither good nor evil."

That very day Iso Thomas talked to Chief Swahini and to Uncle Tula. Uncle Tula was very angry. He threatened all sorts of evil if the sacrifices were not made. But Chief Swahini was beginning to think like Iso Thomas and Mother Nganda, and Ekila and Mpengo, and like the three other Christian families. He was beginning to wonder whether they were right and Uncle Tula was wrong about there being evil spirits who would harm them. He was slowly beginning to believe that God is great and good and wise and loving.

That evening the men met in the chief's house and talked. The second evening they talked some more. But still, they could not agree. Uncle Tula was sure it was best to make sacrifices to the evil spirits. Iso

Thomas kept telling them it wasn't. But when it grew late, Chief Swahini, who had listened till his ears ached, decided that Iso Thomas was right. He said, "Enough! We will not have the dance. We will not make the sacrifices to the evil spirits."

Then Iso Thomas said, "Will you do what the Christian people in my village do?"

"What is that?" asked Chief Swahini. But Uncle Tula went off muttering to talk to Old Tulagi the witch doctor in his house in the dark forest.

"When the gardens are ready for planting," said Iso Thomas, "we gather together. All the men and women and children march out together to the gardens. We hold the seeds in our hands and sing a prayer to God who loves us. We hold up our tools and sing a prayer asking Him to bless them. We ask God to bless the hands with which we make our gardens and do our other work. Then we stand before God and ask Him to bless us in all our ways."

"Yes," said the chief. "I am willing to have you Christian people do that."

The boys in the school became busy at once learning the song of prayer for seedtime. Ekila and her mother taught the girls the song. The Christian women learned it, too. The Christian men heard the others singing it, and they began to learn it.

The Blessing of the Gardens

"What is that?" asked Chief Swahini.

One day, when all was ready, everyone gathered in the village street. The Christian people were dressed in their best and cleanest clothes. Their faces were happy. Chief Swahini went first with Iso Thomas. The children sang as they followed. They sang the Christian songs they had learned at school. But they did not sing the song for the blessing of the seed.

The men and women and children came to the gardens. There in the open spaces in the forest, first at one garden and then at another, they sang the prayer for seedtime. They sang as Iso Thomas had taught them, asking God's blessing on the gardens.

Seeds we bring, Lord, to Thee,
Will Thou bless them, O Lord.
Gardens we bring, Lord, to Thee,
Will Thou bless them, O Lord.
Hands we bring, Lord, to Thee,
Will Thou bless them, O Lord.
Ourselves we bring, Lord, to Thee,
Will Thou bless us, O Lord.

At the end of the last song, Iso Thomas stood and made a prayer. "O God who loves us," he prayed, "help us to come to Thee for help. Help us to know that Thou art great and good and wise and loving. Help us to learn Thy laws of seedtime and growing and harvesting. Help us to know how to work in Thy way. Bless us as this village learns and begins to live in Christian ways. Amen."

8

Learning the Village Ways

It was not long after the time of the blessing of the gardens that the wild elephants began coming through the forest, bothering the villages. The people sent the news from one village to another. They beat on the big hollow-log drums whose sounds carry messages in Africa. Drumbeats came faint but clear to Hidden Village from other villages far away in the forest.

"Listen!" said the people. "The drums are speaking! They are saying that the wild elephants are around."

One night the huge beasts came hunting in the gardens of Chief Swahini's village. They were looking for the food they loved. One of them fell into the pit that the villagers had dug and was killed. The rest were frightened and ran swiftly away.

What excitement for the small boys! An elephant! Mpengo had never seen such great tusks. They would be sold in the downriver town for much money because they were ivory. The ivory belonged to the chief. Chief Swahini would be able to spend the money it brought for new spears and other precious things he wanted. With part of the money that he received, he could pay the tax that Hidden Village had to give each year to the government.

Mpengo watched while the village people took the stiff hair from the elephant's tail. It would be woven into bracelets with clever patterns. Other things would be made from the hide and the tough ears. The meat would make a feast for the whole village.

Mpengo and the other boys worked with the men. "You must learn the knowledge of the men of the forest villages and how they secure food and clothing and the other things that are needed," said Mpengo's father. "There are skillful men in our village. Learn from them everything you can."

Mpengo was glad to learn. He and Mato went with the men whenever they could. They even went along with Uncle Tula when he would let them. Somehow

The meat would make a feast for the whole village.

Mpengo liked Uncle Tula. It was fun to be with him when he was not being angry about the witch doctor business. He knew tricks of hunting; he was skillful with his hands. He could track through the forest as silently as a shadow. Best of all, he was ready to show Mpengo over and over again how a thing should be done.

Iso Thomas watched them one day as they started off on a hunt. He smiled and said softly to Mother Nganda, "Someday Tula will become tired of his witch doctor business. Someday he will understand that it is God who made the world we live in. Someday he will become a Christian. It is good that he and Mpengo are friends. He will listen to what a boy-child says when he will not listen to words from you and me."

"And it is good for Mpengo," said Mother Nganda. "He is learning all the skill of the forest folk. He is learning to love the strong men of my tribe. It is good."

Then she looked down the village street. Ekila was dancing toward them on happy feet. She waved something in the air.

"What can it be?" wondered Mother Nganda aloud.

In no time at all Ekila was there. "Look! Look!" she cried. "Look, O my Mother and my Father, and see what I have!"

They both looked. It was a piece of soft grasscloth. It was woven beautifully, as the women of the village knew how to weave, from the grass that grew on the edges of the swamps.

"Who gave it to you?" asked Mother Nganda, smiling. "Did you return proper thanks?"

"I made it!" Ekila said proudly. "I, myself!"

"What!" said Ekila's mother.

"Is that a true word?" exclaimed her father, looking again at the cloth. "I did not know you could do it. It is difficult to weave soft cloth from the stiff grass."

"The mother of Kamili taught me," said Ekila. "At times when you thought I was playing, we were working. Kamili and I were learning to prepare the grass and weave it. Next we will learn to give the soft brown and black color to some of the grass. Then we can make patterns in our weaving."

"It is very good," said Iso Thomas. "The weaving is good, and I am proud of it. And I am happy, too, that you are learning the skill of the women of this village. For only in the villages of our forest is the grasscloth made in just this way. Our friends, the missionaries, often take pieces of our soft and fine grasscloth to show to their friends in America."

"We can be proud of the things the people of our village can make with their hands," said Mother

Nganda. "Now I am going to the house of the mother of Kamili to thank her for the teaching she has given you."

"You teach Kamili to know about God, and Kamili's mother teaches me how to do fine weaving," said Ekila. "That is good, is it not, my Mother?"

"It is good," agreed her mother. "For when each person gives to the other person the best he knows, life is made better and happier for all. It is the Christian way. I think that the mother of Kamili is walking in the Christian way. And for that, I give thanks to the good God who loves every one of us."

She took the grasscloth in her hand. With Baby Bula on her back and with Ekila skipping along beside her, she went to give thanks to the mother of Kamili and to sit and visit with her for a while.

9

When Little New One Came

It was almost time for the sun to set. The parrots in the trees were squawking and playing. Smoke was going up from the cooking fires in the village.

Then Iso Thomas held up his hand. "Listen," he said.

Mpengo listened. Everyone else in the village was listening, too. Far off could be heard the beating of drums. A message was being sent through the drumbeats.

"A stranger woman, not of our tribe, is traveling in the forest," said the drums. "She has become ill. She has a child with her. The child is ill."

Then the drums were quiet. "Hmmm!" said Iso Thomas. "Those were the drums of our neighbor village. Perhaps that stranger woman will come here. Perhaps she is on her way to our village now."

"No one will want to take her in," said Mother Nganda.

"Why not?" asked Ekila. "Because there is no hospital?"

"No-o-o!" answered her mother. "It is because they are afraid to take in sick strangers. Being afraid keeps people from doing many kind things. It is too bad."

Iso Thomas was right. The sick woman was on the trail to their very own village. She moved slowly as she came down the path. She was so sick she could hardly stand.

The home of Iso Thomas was the first one she came to. Iso saw her from where he sat just inside his door. He and Nganda went out quickly. They helped her walk. She was too ill to speak. She looked at them with mournful eyes. She turned her eyes and looked at her baby. The baby was sick, too.

"Do not worry," said Mother Nganda softly. "I will care for the baby. And we will care for you, too."

A small smile came onto the woman's face. Mother Nganda took the little baby girl. She carried her tenderly and put her into a new basket on a soft piece of old cloth that Ekila brought. "Can you put a few drops of water in her mouth?" Mother Nganda asked

"Do not worry," said Mother Nganda softly.

Ekila. "She is a very sick baby, Ekila. You will have to be very careful."

Ekila nodded. "I will be very careful," she promised.

Mother Nganda went to help the sick mother. Then she came back to help the sick baby. All night, long after Ekila and Mpengo were asleep, the fire burned outside the house of Iso Thomas. The sick woman lay on a sleeping mat they had carried out. She had a sickness they did not dare take into the house with the children. Iso and Nganda took loving care of her. They did everything they could to help her. But before morning the sick woman died, and there was only the little sick baby left.

When the village people came in the morning to carry the body of the baby's mother out into the forest, they wanted to take the baby, too. "We will just leave it with its dead mother," said an old, old woman. When Mother Nganda would not give up the baby, the old one asked, "What else is there to do?"

"I will care for the baby. I think maybe I can make her well," said Mother Nganda.

Uncle Tula came along last. He scowled. "It will bring bad luck to the village," he said in a cross voice.

Iso Thomas laughed. "No! No!" he answered. "To do something good can never bring bad luck. To do good is to act like children of God."

But the old witch doctor, who was Tula's father, had told the people such stories of bad luck that Chief Swahini was frightened. He made Iso Thomas and Mother Nganda and Mpengo and Ekila and Baby Bula and little New One move out of the village. They had to go into an old hut at the edge of the gardens.

Ekila cried. "I hate this village," she said. "They are unkind to us. Let us go back to our own old home."

Mpengo sat on a log scowling. "Do we have to keep that sick one?" he asked.

Iso Thomas sat on another old log. There were no little stools here such as he had made for use in their village home.

"Would you be the person to carry the little New One out into the forest and leave her where the wild animals could carry her off?" asked Iso Thomas, smiling a little.

"No. Not I!" said Mpengo in a hurry.

"Could Ekila do it?"

"No," said Ekila, not waiting for anyone else to answer for her.

"Do you think your mother would do it?"

"Never, not ever," said both children.

"Or I?"

"Not you," they said.

Their father smiled. "That is what your mother and I thought. We are Christians. We could not possibly put a little New One, even though she is sick, out into the dark forest to die. Be patient, my children. When the little New One gets well and is a chubby, laughing baby, the village will ask us to come back. They will learn that there is nothing to fear. They will see what the loving way can do."

And that is just what happened. For the sickness of the little New One was a baby sickness that Mother Nganda knew exactly how to treat. Before long it was over, and little New One smiled. Then she began to gurgle and coo, like babies do all over the world.

Baby Bula would toddle over to the basket where little New One lay and poke her with his finger. Ekila would dangle a ball made of grass roots in front of her to make her laugh. Mpengo went into the forest and shot a little animal and brought home the skin to help make a soft bed for the stranger baby.

"Can we keep her?" asked Ekila one day.

"Surely," said Iso Thomas. "She will be a new little sister for you."

Then one day Uncle Tula came past. "The chief says, and he told me to tell you, that you may come home again," said Uncle Tula.

"Truly?" asked Iso Thomas.

"Truly," said Uncle Tula. "No harm has come to the

village. The strange child is well. The fathers want you to come back and have school again for the children."

"Ah!" said Iso Thomas.

"Also," said Uncle Tula with a slow smile, "everyone misses Iso Thomas and his family. Everyone wants them back again."

"Good," said Iso Thomas. "We will come."

Then Uncle Tula looked into the treetops. "Is there a small boy who would like to go hunting?" he asked.

Mpengo jumped to his feet with a shout.

"I!" he cried. "I!"

Uncle Tula grinned. "Come, then." They started away. "The village is ashamed that it listened to Grandfather Witch Doctor," he said to Iso Thomas, talking over his shoulder. "Chief Swahini is ashamed that he did not follow the Christian teaching. Go back, and they will listen with ears that are more open than before," he said, and vanished into the forest with Mpengo.

10

A Visit from the Missionary

Months slipped by. One day Iso said, "It is time for the mission people to come visiting the faraway villages. The village drums will tell us when they are coming close to us."

Mpengo danced with joy. Ekila skipped and clapped her hands. Baby Bula clapped his hands and gurgled. Little New One in her basket chuckled softly, as if she understood that everyone was happy.

Mother Nganda began to think about the food she would prepare for the visitors.

"When will they get here?" asked Mpengo eagerly.

"Who knows exactly?" said his father. "The steamer with Captain John will bring White Doctor and the others up the river. Then they will go on foot through the forest from one village to another. In one village they will stay one day, in another two, in some, perhaps longer."

"What will they do when they are here?" asked Ekila.

"They will talk with the preacher-teacher or the nurse or the schoolteacher who lives in each village."

"A schoolteacher just like you," interrupted Mpengo.

"Just like me," agreed his father. "They will listen to what the children have learned."

"Here, too?" asked Ekila.

"Here, too," said Iso. "They will talk to the chief and give teaching to the village people, especially to those who want to become Christians. If there are some whose hearts are ready to follow Jesus, they will baptize them," added Iso.

Far away a drum sounded. Everyone stopped to listen to what the drum said.

"The Christian people come. The white man comes. A white child comes!" beat out the drums.

"A white child!" shouted Mpengo. "It will be Tommy!"

"Do not be too sure," said his father. But he smiled at Mpengo's happiness.

It was early the next afternoon that Iso Thomas and Chief Swahini went down the trail to meet the visitors.

A Visit from the Missionary

Mpengo and Mato crept along behind the menfolk.

At last, they saw the travelers. There along the forest trail, under the dancing shadows of the great trees, came the visitors.

"Big Inkema!" shouted Mpengo. "And Tommy!"

Inkema raised a long spear in greeting and smiled but did not speak.

"Sh!" said Mato. "It is not proper for children to speak first."

Mpengo jumped up on a log. "Yi!" he whispered excitedly. "It *is* Tommy. My friend, Tommy."

Neither Mato nor Mpengo paid much attention to all the polite talk of their elders. Tommy spied Mpengo and squirmed around the edge of the trail toward them. He could speak Mpengo's language as well as his own, and soon the three boys were off on their own affairs.

"So many, many things," said Mpengo, "there are for you to see!"

When they went to see the elephant pit, Tommy almost fell in, it was hidden so carefully. Mpengo and Mato grabbed him. "Be careful!" they shouted. "We do not wish to have you with broken bones!"

Soon the visitors were in the village. Inkema and Dr. White, who was a doctor missionary, were busy looking

"Be careful!" they shouted.

at the sick people. They treated many sicknesses. They heard about Iso Thomas teaching the children how to be healthy. They looked at the babies of the village and heard how little New One had been saved. They praised the mothers who had taken care of their babies in the good ways that Mother Nganda had taught them.

There was much talk with Chief Swahini and with the men of the village. "If anyone is very sick or breaks bones," said Dr. White, "Iso will be able to give first aid. Then put your sick or injured person in a canoe with fast and strong paddlers. Bring him down the river to the Christian hospital."

"That is many days' journey," said the chief.

"Better several days' journey than many years of being a cripple," said Inkema.

"True words!" said a quiet voice behind them.

Iso did not turn around. He knew that voice. It was the voice of Tula. There was gladness in Iso's heart. Tula was speaking like a friend.

That evening the family of Iso and the three Christian families of the village and the visitors had a worship service. It was not held inside a church. As yet there was no church. It was under the roof where the children had school each day. The roof was on poles, and the walls came up just high enough to keep dust and leaves from blowing across the floor.

All the people of the village crowded in. When there was no more room, they sat outside the low walls and looked in.

Mpengo saw a face peering over the wall at the back. It was the face of Uncle Tula. Mpengo whispered to Tommy who sat beside him, "Look, there is my Uncle Tula. His father, who is also my grandfather, is the old witch doctor. Tula has been very angry because we came. Now he is becoming friendly."

"Does he listen to the Christian teaching?" asked Tommy. He liked Uncle Tula's face. "He looks as if he would make a good friend," said Tommy.

"Never before has he come to hear the Christian teaching," said Mpengo. "But he asks me many questions when we are off in the forest."

Then the boys were quiet, for the meeting had begun. They sang the hymns that Christian people all over the world sing. Tommy sang them in the language of the forest folk. "Hymns are the same," he said to Mpengo, "in this village and in the big church in America where we used to worship."

Iso read from the Bible. He read from a copy printed in the language of the people.

Dr. White preached. He had learned the language of the forest folk. He talked to them in words they could understand. He helped them to live more like Jesus.

A Visit from the Missionary

He told them how God wants people to live.

Then Inkema prayed a prayer to God. He thanked God for His love. He asked God's blessing on all the people of the whole wide world. He asked God to help people to live in Jesus' way and be more kind and loving and helpful and true every single day.

After the service was over, Inkema talked to the Christian families. He talked to other village people who were thinking about becoming followers of Jesus.

At last, it was bedtime. Early the next morning the visitors would go on.

Mato crept up to Dr. White who was sitting in a place near the fire. "White Doctor," he said.

Dr. White smiled at him. "What question have you to ask, Mato?" he said.

"Let me become a doctor like you," begged Mato.

Dr. White looked at Mato's shiny eyes and eager face. "To be a doctor takes much learning," he said slowly. "First, learn all you can from Iso. He can teach you much, right here in your village. Then, if your father is willing, you can come to the mission school where the hospital is. When that is finished, if you are learning well, we will talk about your becoming a doctor."

Mato's father, Chief Swahini, listened to Dr. White's words. "Is it possible," he muttered to himself, "that my son should become a healer of sick people?"

11

Big-Fish-Catching Day

"Soon," said Mato, "comes the big-fish-catching day."

"What is that?" asked Mpengo. After almost a year in Hidden Village, he still had a lot to learn about forest ways.

"All the village people go to Big Swamp Lagoon. It is a long way up the trail. The men cut the dike they put in last year," Mato explained. "Then the water runs slowly out."

"And then what?"

"We all go into the swamp, the men and the women and the children. The fish begin to flop around in the shallow water, and we catch them. We put them into baskets. Then we bring them home and smoke them."

All year we eat them," said Mato. "But it is the time of catching them that is fun."

Mpengo and Ekila could hardly wait for the big-fish-catching day. Their father was going and so was their mother. She would put Baby Bula and little New One on the bank. Then she would wade in along with the rest of the family and catch fish in her newly woven baskets.

The big day came. But when the whole village arrived at Big Swamp Lagoon, there was no dike, no water, no fish! People from some other village had come and stolen the fish. The men and some of the women and boys went to another smaller pool, but it was too far for Ekila and Mother Nganda and Baby Bula and New One.

That evening there were only a few fish to smoke, and everyone was angry. Food is very important where there are no stores. "What shall we eat at the end of the year?" asked the womenfolk.

The young hunters said nothing. By the next morning, they had disappeared. Uncle Tula had disappeared, too.

"Where have they gone?" asked Mpengo.

"I think," said Mato, "that they have gone to Big Bend Village. They think those people stole our fish. So they are going to steal them back."

Sure enough! On the third day, the young men came back with the fish, already neatly smoked. But they also had some beautiful new grasscloth and some brand-new spears and baskets.

"That is not good," said Iso Thomas.

"Why not?" asked Chief Swahini.

"It is not the right thing to do. Because they stole our fish is no reason for us to steal their cloth and spears and baskets. Stealing is bad."

The young men listened, but they did not like what Iso Thomas said. They had their own ideas. They did not agree that taking the grasscloth and new spears was wrong.

"We have always fought with the people of Big Bend Village," one said. "They belong to another tribe. First, they steal something from us. Then, we steal something from them."

Another young man spoke up. "They are sure to come now and try to steal something from us," he said. "Let us dig big holes in the path, like the pit we dug for the elephants. Then if those people come to steal, they will fall in."

"Many people use the paths. Friendly people of our own tribe use them," said Tula. "We do not want to catch them in a pit. They would be very angry."

"We will guard the pits during the day. Friends travel by daylight," said the young men. "The people from Big Bend Village will come to steal in the dark. If they fall in, they will be caught."

Iso Thomas said nothing more to the young men. It was no use. They were going to do just what they wanted anyway.

So the pits were dug in all the paths leading to the village. By day the young men guarded the pits to warn travelers to go around them. But at night they left them ready to catch unfriendly visitors.

Iso was very unhappy about it all. "Someone might get hurt. Then there would be war between our villages. Let us live in peace," he said to Chief Swahini.

The chief wanted peace between the villages. He knew how much better it was to live as friends. So, at last, he agreed that Iso Thomas might go to Big Bend Village with a message from Chief Swahini.

It was the first time Iso had left his family alone in Hidden Village. He called Mpengo and Ekila to him.

"If anything happens while I am gone," he said, "try to think what is the Christian way to act. Then be brave and do what is right." He patted each of them on the shoulder. "Take care of your mother and the little ones," he said.

"We will," promised Mpengo and Ekila.

They watched their father walking along the forest trail until he was out of sight.

12

The Broken Leg

Two days went by. One evening Mpengo and Mato stayed out fishing too long. Because they had to hurry home, they forgot all about the pits in the pathways. Mato, who was hurrying ahead, stepped right into one.

Down he went. Crash!

"Mato! Mato! Has harm come to you?" called Mpengo, looking down through the broken branches into the pit. But Mato only groaned. Mpengo knew he was badly hurt from the sound he made.

It seemed a long time before Mpengo could get back with helpers from Hidden Village. When they got Mato out of the pit, they found that his leg was broken.

He moaned as they moved him even though they did it carefully. Iso Thomas had taught them how to make a sort of stretcher, and they quickly made one and took Mato to the village.

"Where is Iso?" asked Chief Swahini. Then he remembered. Iso was not yet back from Big Bend Village. "There is no one else who knows what to do!" said Chief Swahini. "My son, my son! He will be a cripple all his days."

"Call the witch doctor," muttered the old, old women. "He will know what to do."

Chief Swahini shrugged his shoulders. "Since when can the witch doctor make a crooked leg straight?" said he.

But no one knew what else to do, and at last a messenger went hurrying to the thick woods to call Old Tulagi, the witch doctor. His hut was hidden away among the bushes there.

Mato groaned as he lay with his twisted broken leg. Mpengo squatted beside him in the firelight. Off at one side stood Uncle Tula, a queer look on his face.

Mpengo looked from the face of Chief Swahini to the faces of the old, old women. His father had often said that it was the old people who were most afraid to try new ways. Would these old ones insist on doing

Old Tulagi slipped into the firelight.

what the witch doctor said? How Mpengo wished his father would come!

Old Tulagi, the witch doctor, slipped into the firelight, quiet as a shadow. He shook his magic rattle. He looked at Mato lying on the ground. He muttered words beneath his breath.

"Can you cure my son?" demanded Chief Swahini.

"Who knows!" The witch doctor bent over Mato. "You have not made offerings for a long time to the spirits who live in the forest."

Chief Swahini said nothing. It was quite true. He did not really believe anymore that there were spirits in the forest. It was only because Iso Thomas was not there that he had agreed to see what Old Tulagi could do.

Mpengo's face was full of trouble. He knew that a long time ago when little Yoka broke his leg, the witch doctor had dug a hole in the ground and had put Yoka's leg into it and covered it with earth. Then he had built a fire over it and said charms. Yoka's leg was burned, and now he was a cripple who could not stand up but had to crawl wherever he went.

Surely Old Tulagi would not do that to Mato.

But that was exactly what Old Tulagi was planning to do. The Christian men and women of the three families and Mother Nganda begged Chief Swahini not to let Old Tulagi use his treatment.

"Do as White Doctor said. We will help carry Mato to the river and down to the mission hospital," said the men.

"Wait until morning. Iso Thomas will be back," begged Mother Nganda.

All the time Uncle Tula stood looking on, saying never a word. Old Tulagi, with his white-painted face and his leopard skin and his charm-rattles and his mutterings, paid no attention. He went right on with his witch doctor business.

The hole was dug. Mato was placed so his leg could be stretched out in it. The men began to fill the earth in around it.

"No! No!" begged Mpengo. "He will be crippled like little Yoka. Wait till my father comes."

Old Tulagi roared at him. He knew that if Iso Thomas arrived, there would be no chance for him.

Mpengo knelt by Mato. "Do not let them, Mato. Make them take you down the river to the mission hospital."

"Quiet!" said Chief Swahini. "Shall a small boy tell the chief what to do?"

"Not a small boy, O Chief," said another voice. "Listen to my words." It was Uncle Tula! "New days have come to this village. We are learning new ways. Let the boy be

The Broken Leg

taken to the mission hospital. One of those men who traveled with White Doctor told me that he had had his leg broken. In three places it was broken. But he was taken to the hospital, and today he walks straight and strong."

Old Tulagi muttered angrily.

Chief Swahini looked from him to Tula. After all, Tula had planned to be a witch doctor and knew all about the charms. If he thought it was better to go to the hospital—

Uncle Tula was speaking again. "I will go with the boy. I will stay with him till his leg is well."

Mpengo listened with wondering ears. Uncle Tula was a friend. He was speaking just as Iso Thomas would have spoken.

Chief Swahini's face became happier. "I will send Mato if you will take him," he said. "We will try the Christian way."

Old Tulagi knew he was beaten. He slipped away into the forest. He began to wonder what the Christian teaching really was. He began to think he had better find out something about it. If his own son Tula thought it was better than witch doctoring, he had better listen to some of the teachings himself.

13

THE JOURNEY TO THE MISSION

As soon as Old Tulagi had gone, Mother Nganda came and put a splint on the leg that was broken. She knew many things about caring for sickness and accidents.

"Uncle Tula," begged Mpengo, "let me go with you!"

Uncle Tula looked at him thoughtfully. "If your mother is willing, you may go," he said at last.

"Who will go with me to carry Mato on a stretcher through the forest? Who will help paddle the canoe?" asked Uncle Tula.

"We will," said the fathers in the three Christian families.

"It will be a long, hard trip. We must get there quickly," said Uncle Tula. "Will anyone else help?"

"If we leave the village," said one of the young men, "our enemies from Big Bend Village may attack it while we are gone."

Chief Swahini spoke. "Iso Thomas has taken a message of peace to Big Bend Village. I do not think they will come. I have offered to return the spears and the baskets."

The young men frowned and grumbled. But one of them said, "Good! It will be more exciting to take a trip to the mission hospital than to fight our neighbors. I will go with Tula. I will help paddle the canoe."

Three other young men said they would go, too.

So they began busily, in the dancing firelight, to get ready. A stretcher must be made to carry Mato. Food must be prepared. Chief Swahini said he would send two extra men to carry the elephant tusks as far as the canoe. The tusks would be taken to the government office beyond the mission station to be sold for much money.

"I will pay to have my son healed with part of the money that I get for the tusks," said Chief Swahini proudly. He made ready a gift of cunningly woven bracelets of elephant hair for White Doctor.

Mother Nganda said that Mpengo might go, and he,

too, made ready. Ekila gathered a bundle of food and put some clean clothes in a package for him.

"It will be easier for Mato if you are along," said Mpengo's mother. "You can sit beside him in the canoe and give him food and water. You can see that the banana leaf stays in place and shields him from the hot sun."

That night the people had only a few hours' sleep. Very, very early, the women went out to the gardens and cut banana leaves. The men would use them to make a shelter so that the hot sun would not shine on Mato while he lay in the bottom of the canoe. Mato's leg was hurting. He would have much pain during the trip.

Before long the travelers were off. The stretcher was slung like a hammock from a pole. Four men carried it. The other four changed places with them one at a time, so as not to stop moving. The two men carrying the elephant tusks followed. Mpengo trotted along behind. They went just as fast as they could.

"It is a good thing that I have spent so much time on the forest trails with Uncle Tula," thought Mpengo. "A year ago I would have had to rest again and again." There was no resting this time, and Mpengo was hot and very tired before the stream was reached.

The people of the friendly village at the fork of the

The Journey to the Mission

There was no resting this time.

stream came hurrying from their houses. They were surprised when they saw Mato. They thought it very strange that he was being taken on a journey. "Why not call the witch doctor?" they asked.

"The Christian way is better," said Tula. "The leg will heal straight and strong."

He and the other men carefully put Mato into a big dugout canoe. They made banana leaves into a shelter over him. Mpengo sat close beside him, to give him drinks of water. Mato was too sick to want food.

"Hurry!" said Tula. "We must get to the doctor with all speed."

The elephant tusks were loaded into the canoe. The two men who had carried them pushed the canoe out. The paddles were lifted high by the eight paddlers. Uncle Tula started a paddlers' song to keep the paddles working together.

Because they were going downstream, the current was strong. It helped them to go fast. By night they should reach the Luapa River. Then three days' paddling downstream would bring them to the hospital.

The sun was ready to set when the canoe, with its tired paddlers, shot out into the broad waters of the Luapa. Mpengo gave a shout. There, tied up to the beach, was the mission steamer, waiting as if it had expected them.

"It is Captain John! It is Captain John!" said

Mpengo. "He will take us in one day to the mission hospital because the current will help carry us along."

And so he did. The canoe was towed behind the steamer with two men in it to steer it. Captain John went downriver as fast as was safe. He sent a message ahead by the drums. "I bring a boy with a broken leg. Get ready. Get ready," beat out the drums, from one village to another.

It was dark when the mission station was reached. Great bonfires had been lit on the beach to help them come in and tie the steamer. White Doctor and Big Inkema were there waiting. Nurse Eoto and Mark Mpoku were ready to help.

Mato was carried up to the hospital. Bright electric lights shone while Dr. White set his leg. Uncle Tula, holding his spear, stood by to watch. Mpengo was there, too.

"Wonderful!" said Uncle Tula. "This must be magic! What have you done so that Mato feels no pain while you work?"

"No magic," said Inkema. "It is a medicine that is found in God's good world. He has given men wisdom to use it."

That night Mpengo slept at the house of his father's father, who lived nearby. Mato, for the first time in his life, slept in a bed.

Uncle Tula and the paddlers were taken to a house on the edge of the mission station. But Tula did not stay there. He slept on the floor beside Mato.

"Chief Swahini gave him to me to bring here. I will stay by him," said Uncle Tula.

14

At the Mission Station

When the ivory was sold, the paddlers went back in their canoe to tell Chief Swahini of the safe journey.

All the people of Hidden Village gathered to hear. "And so Mato rests comfortably in the Christian hospital. His leg will mend straight and strong. In two moons we are to go back to the Luapa River to fetch him home," said the paddlers.

Chief Swahini sat contentedly by his fire, listening to them.

His heart was happy because of the news about Mato. "That is good!" said he. "I see more and more that the Christian ways are good ways."

Then he told the paddlers the news of what had happened at home. He told them how Iso Thomas had made peace with Big Bend Village. "We can fill up the traps in the paths," said Chief Swahini. "No longer will the pits be a danger to our children and to strangers. We are at peace with our neighbors."

Meanwhile, Uncle Tula was being shown what was going on at the mission hospital. He was seeing all sorts of things, such as he had never even heard of before. Each day Mpengo took him around the mission station. Each evening Tula sat by Mato in the hospital and told what he had seen.

"I have seen White Doctor make little black marks on a white paper," said Tula. "The paper I took to Big Inkema's house. Inkema looked at it. He laughed and gave me two oranges!"

"That is reading and writing," said Mpengo. "Like we did on our sand table at the school in our village, Mato. It is no different, except that we had no paper."

"There is a big machine that roars and chatters," said Uncle Tula. "It eats paper and spits it out."

Mpengo smiled. "That is the mission printing press," he said. "It makes books like the Bible and the hymnbook my father had."

Uncle Tula visited the sawmill where the great trees were cut into lumber to build houses. He saw the little village where the leper people stayed. He saw how lovingly the Christian people cared for them. He was filled with wonder.

But most of all Tula was surprised when he went to church. Never had he seen so many people gathering together with happy faces and spotless, clean clothes. Mpengo had invited Tula to go with him to the service.

Uncle Tula carried his spear. Mpengo tried to get him to leave it outside. But Big Inkema heard and said, "Let him take it in, Mpengo. His heart is not yet ready to leave his spear outside. He is still just a little bit afraid. Soon, I think, he will not be afraid anymore. Then he will be willing to leave his spear. He will be ready to go into the church without it."

So they went into the church. Mpengo was filled with happiness to be among his friends again. He sang the hymns and prayed the prayers and listened to the wise words of the pastor.

One Sunday a few weeks later, Mato came to church, too. He hobbled in on crutches. He could join in the singing. He could join in the prayers.

So the days slipped by. Uncle Tula and Mato talked often about the way in which everyone lived in peace. No spears. No shields. "It is a good way to live," said Uncle Tula.

At last, the time came when White Doctor called

Uncle Tula carried his spear.

Mato and Mpengo and Tula to his office. He looked at Mato's leg.

"It is well," he said. "Tomorrow Captain John starts up the river with the mission steamer. You may go with him."

Mato's eyes became bright and shining. Everyone had been good to him, but he was getting just a little bit homesick. He wanted to go home.

Uncle Tula smiled. He wanted to get back and tell the people of the village all he had seen. He wanted to tell about all that he had heard. Then, too, he was going to ask Iso Thomas to tell him more about Christian teachings. Already Tula had become a Christian in his heart. He would learn more. Then he could be baptized, and everyone would know he was a Christian. How glad Iso Thomas would be! How glad Tula's sister Nganda would be!

Mpengo was so happy he just could not stay still. He danced for joy. He wanted to get home to Hidden Village. He wanted to see his father and mother. He could hardly wait to see Ekila and Brother Bula, who could not be called Baby anymore, and little New One.

"Tomorrow! Tomorrow! Tomorrow we go home!" sang Mpengo and Mato. And in his heart, Uncle Tula sang it, too.

Someday, when they were older, Mpengo and Mato intended to come back to the mission hospital. They both wanted to become doctors. If they could not be doctors, they would learn to be nurses. Big Inkema was learning to be a nurse. Men nurses could go into far-off villages where the women nurses could not go. But right now, Mpengo and Mato were still small boys. Hidden Village was the place where they wanted most of all to be.

15

At Home in Hidden Village

What happiness there was in the village when Uncle Tula and Mpengo and Mato came home! All the boys went running down the trail to meet them. All the people were out in the village street to welcome them.

The people of the village looked and looked at Mato. They could hardly believe their eyes. His leg that had been so broken and crooked was straight and clean and strong. Mato could run and jump. He had walked all the way from the friendly village where the trail started.

Chief Swahini had a feast in honor of the great day. All the good things that African mothers know how to cook and that African boys and girls like to eat were ready.

Everyone ate together. The men and boys first. And then the women and girls. That is the traditional way in the Congo forest.

Everyone was there. Even the old witch doctor came. He left his charms behind him. He wanted to hear what his son Tula had to tell about the place where he had been.

Mpengo looked around with eyes that saw things in a new way. He suddenly noticed that the houses and yards were cleaner. Voices were happier. He heard more laughing and less quarreling. And often a man would come by with no spear in his hand.

"It is because we are at peace with Big Bend Village and our other neighbors," said Iso Thomas.

"And because the people of Hidden Village are beginning to live in the Christian way," said Mother Nganda.

The moonlight streamed down on the village after the feast was over. Ekila and the other little girls played dancing and clapping games in the white moonlight.

Mpengo and Mato sat with the other boys, telling them all about the mission station.

Uncle Tula was with Chief Swahini and Iso Thomas and Old Tulagi and the other men talking and talking and talking.

At Home in Hidden Village 89

Mpengo and Mato sat with the other boys.

Mother Nganda sat with the women. They kept their babies and little children close beside them.

"Our village is a different place these days," said the mother of Kamili. "It is a better and happier place."

"To hear you say those words makes me glad," said Mother Nganda. "It is a happy thing when the people of a village begin to live in the Christian way."

"True words," said Kamili's mother. "You and your family have shown our village what the Christian way is." She reached out and patted little New One lovingly on the shoulder.

There was happiness everywhere in Hidden Village.